2004

Uściski i pocałunki
dla Ramosi,
Osiee

D1809576

For Mother

Written and Illustrated
by

Lynne Gerard

The C.R. Gibson Company · Norwalk, Ct. 06856

Sometimes
it's a familiar
fragrance,
or a certain way
the sunlight
brightens a room,
or maybe
it's the mood
of a particular song
that triggers
a memory
and makes my
heart warm as
I think of
you.

Somehow,
  for some reason,
  you and I
    have always
  had a
  special closeness
    and
  understanding.

Sure, there
were times when
we rubbed each
other the wrong
way and
said things we
really didn't
mean ...

but that
happens to everyone
at one time
or another
and even so,
I always
felt loved.

I can
remember the
times I was sick
and you would
make me comfortable
in many small
ways and help
me get well ...
and I
would
feel loved.

When
I was afraid,
you would soothe me
in your calm
mother's way
and the
fear would be gone...
and I would
feel loved.

If ever
I was down,
you would always
know and you
would talk to me
and understand me...
and I would
feel loved.

When I
would attempt
to try
something
new,
you would
lend me
your guidance
and support...
and I
would feel
loved.

And,
when I
succeeded at
even the smallest
thing, you were
my biggest
admirer
with the biggest smile...
and I
would
feel loved

There were times
when you would
cook my favorite
meal, or
bring me a
treat from
the
store,

for no
special
reason ...
and I
would
feel
loved .

You took
an interest
in my life;
you
cared about
who I was and
you respected
my individuality...
these are
precious
things.

Now
that I am
older,
I realize
what a tremendous
responsibility
it is
to be
a
mother.

There are
sleepless nights,
times of
worry and
periods of
frustration.

A mother
feels her child's
pain
deeper than
if it were
her own.

A mother
loses a bit
of her individuality
as the
concerns of
her child come
before her
own.

A mother
will go
without
to make sure
that her child
has the
very best.

As I think
back on the
many things you
did that
made me
feel loved,
I wonder,
have I ever
taken time
to do the same
for you?

I hope
there were times
when I
stopped thinking
about my
world long enough
to wonder about
yours.

I hope
I didn't miss
chances
to listen
to you
and
speak
an encouraging
word.

Now
is a good
time to tell
you that you
have been
a terrific
mother.

I want you
to know
how much I
appreciate
you.
I
appreciate
you for all
the love I
have forgotten.

and all the
love I
remember
and all the
love we
have yet
to share.

And when something
special touches
you with a
memory of me,
I hope you will
feel loved ...

because
I love you
Mom!